Marion Public Library
1095 6th Avenue
Marion, IA 52302-3428
(319) 377-3412

HOW TO SURVIVE IN THE WILDERNESS

BY SAMANTHA BELL

The Child's World®

Published by The Child's World®
1980 Lookout Drive • Mankato, MN 56003-1705
800-599-READ • www.childsworld.com

Acknowledgments
The Child's World®: Mary Berendes, Publishing Director
Red Line Editorial: Editorial direction and production
The Design Lab: Design
Photographs ©: Shutterstock Images, cover, 1, 5, 17, 19;
Mendocino County Sheriff's Department/AP Images,
7; Jean-Christophe Bott/Keystone/AP Images, 9;
Robert Cicchetti/Shutterstock Images, 11; M. Cornelius/
Shutterstock Images, 13; Dan Collier/Shutterstock
Images, 15; Dudarev Mikhail/Shutterstock Images, 21

ISBN 9781609731601
LCCN 2014959921

Printed in the United States of America
Mankato, MN
July, 2015
PA02260

ABOUT THE AUTHOR

Samantha Bell lives in South Carolina with her husband, four children, and lots of animals. She has written and illustrated more than 30 books, from picture books for kids to nonfiction for older students. She loves spending time in nature but always has lots of supplies on hand.

TABLE OF CONTENTS

CHAPTER ONE

WAITING FOR HELP

In September 2013, 72-year-old Gene Penaflor went hunting with a friend in a California forest. The two men went in different directions to track deer. They planned to meet for lunch. But Penaflor never came back.

Penaflor had walked about 2.5 miles (4 km). He had not planned to go so far from the road. Suddenly, he slipped down a steep hill and hit his head hard. The impact knocked him unconscious.

When Penaflor awoke, he noticed he had a bad cut on his chin. But he had not broken any bones. He was not sure what time it was. A thick fog had rolled in. He did not know how to get back.

Penaflor knew he needed to stay in the area. He might never be found if he kept wandering. But he

It rained when Penaflor was in the woods. He crawled under a big log to stay dry.

PROTEIN

Your body needs protein to stay strong. Protein is the body's main building block for muscles, bones, hair, skin, and nails. It also helps the body fight against germs and organisms that can cause disease. In the wilderness, people can get protein by eating eggs, insects, fish, turtles, birds, and mammals.

was high in the mountains. It was cold. He went downhill to set up camp but did not go any farther.

Penaflor had lost his knife but still had his rifle. He would need to get everything else from nature. He found a stream where he could get water. He was able to light a fire. Days passed. Sometimes the temperature was below freezing. He put grass and leaves around his body for **insulation**.

Penaflor was too tired and weak to hunt large animals. But he shot squirrels and other small game with his gun. He ate lizards, frogs, and snakes that he caught. He scooped up algae from the water and ate that, too.

Finally, after 19 days, a hunter wandered close to Penaflor's camp. Penaflor saw him and called for help.

The hunter heard him and came to help. Penaflor was hungry, weak, and tired. But he was safe.

It can be fun to experience nature through outdoor activities. Camping, hiking, skiing, rafting, and rock climbing offer lots of adventure. But nature is unpredictable. You should always be prepared for an emergency. That way, if disaster does strike, you will be ready to survive in the wilderness.

More than 100 people went out to look for Penaflor the day after he went missing.

CHAPTER TWO

KEYS TO SURVIVAL

People have to survive in the wilderness for different reasons. Some people get lost. Like Penaflor, they might become confused and not be able to find their way back. Other times, people get caught in natural disasters like storms and avalanches. Sometimes, an accident will leave them stranded.

Supplies and outdoor skills can help a person survive in the wilderness. But the most important thing to have is a good attitude. People who are lost need to stay confident that they will get out.

In July 2003, Amy Racina was hiking by herself in the King's Canyon National Park in California. She walked off the trail near a **ravine**. The ground suddenly crumbled beneath her. Racina fell a long way down.

Many people bring electronic signals into the mountains. These can help rescuers find the hikers if something goes wrong.

She landed on some rocks. She broke both of her legs and one of her hips. But she did not give up. She pulled herself along with her hands for four days until some other hikers found her.

It is important to evaluate the situation when stuck in the wilderness. If you are lost, stay where you are. People are harder to find if they walk around. Move only if you need to find a safer location. If you must move, it is good to go to a place easy for rescuers to see.

Sometimes people know the way out of the wilderness. But it takes them a while to get there. They might be hurt. Or it might be getting dark. In 1992, 25-year-old Colby Coombs was climbing Mount Foraker in Alaska. Before he reached the top, he was caught in an avalanche. He broke his ankle, shoulder blade, and two bones in his neck. It took him five days to get back down the mountain.

To survive in the wilderness, the first thing to do is build a shelter. A shelter helps protect from the sun, wind, rain, and snow. There are many different kinds of shelter.

Coombs had a tent with him. But a shelter can also be simple. An **evergreen** tree can protect you from wind or rain. In 2009, nine-year-old Grayson Wynne was separated from his family in Ashley National Forest. He remembered some survival tips he learned from a television show. Grayson created a small shelter under a fallen tree to keep himself dry.

People lost in the woods can use branches and sticks to create strong shelters.

Sometimes survivors need extra warmth. Penaflor used leaves for insulation. But there are other ways to keep warm. In August 2014, 58-year-old Mike Vilhauer went fishing with friends. He wandered off to find grasshoppers to use as fishing bait. But he could not find his way back. The first two nights, he covered himself with pine needles and bark to stay warm. After that, he found a large rock to use as a shelter.

A sturdier shelter like a lean-to takes longer to set up. You can make one of these by forming a frame with larger branches and covering it with sticks or leaves. These kinds of shelters seem more like a home. They often help people keep a good attitude.

Snow is another good insulator. In a cold climate, you can dig a cave into a **snowdrift**. The cave should be big enough to lie down in. Grass, leaves, and brush on the floor of the cave can keep you off the snow.

In addition to a shelter, survivors often need a fire to stay warm. People use several different kinds of fuel to make fire. Tinder is thin, dry material that is easy to light. Bark, dry grass, and pine needles make good tinder. Kindling is a little bigger. Kindling consists of thin, dry branches about as thick as a pencil. Kindling helps the flame grow. Once there is a good flame, smaller branches can be added. Finally, larger branches are used to keep the fire burning. Dead branches from standing trees are best. Wood that has been sitting on the ground is often **damp** or wet.

Some people surround fires with stones, clay, or mud. This helps keep the fire from getting out of control.

TYPES OF WOOD FOR A FIRE

There are many types of trees in the wilderness. Evergreens like cedar, spruce, and pine are softwood trees. Softwood trees usually contain sap. This makes the wood burn more quickly and give off more smoke than hardwood trees. Rescuers can easily spot smoky fires. Most trees with broad leaves, such as hickory, beech, and oak, have harder wood. It is often more difficult to light hardwoods. But they last longer. They also make hot coals that can be used later.

Once a survivor has a fire, the next thing to do is find water to drink. People can live only a few days without water. It is always good to **purify** water, even if only through a cloth. But you may need to drink water that is not completely clean. Staying **hydrated** is more important than avoiding unclean water.

Water moves downhill, so low areas will likely have a stream or small pool. People in colder areas can melt snow or ice. Others gather water when it rains.

In 2011, 40-year-old Bill Lawrence was hunting with friends when he got lost. His water ran out. But he was able to catch rainwater in his water bottle.

People lose water quickly when they are hiking. Finding a source of water is very important.

There is also water in the ground. You can look for places where the plants are bright green and dig there. Animals also need water. Tracks are another sign that water is close. After Lawrence drank his rainwater, he followed animal tracks and found a puddle.

CHAPTER THREE

DAILY TASKS

People can live for weeks without eating. But they will become weaker and weaker without food. It is always good to bring extra food into the wilderness. Trail mix is an easy, lightweight option that contains lots of energy. It is usually made up of nuts, seeds, dried fruit, and chocolate. Beef jerky and energy bars are other good foods to take hiking.

You may have to get your food from nature if you do not have any supplies to eat. It is important for people going into the wilderness to learn what they can eat in the area. That way, they do not eat something that will make them sick.

People in the wilderness often find fruit near their campsites. Lawrence ate **persimmons** he found on the

Deadly nightshade berries look similar to blueberries but are poisonous.

ground. Berries are common, too. But some plants are poisonous. Avoid eating any unfamiliar plants.

Survivors can also search for animals to eat. Lawrence found some worms under a stump and ate them. Grasshoppers, crickets, and termites can be good to eat. Insects that have bright colors or give off a strong smell are not usually good to eat. Do not eat any animal unless you know that eating it will not harm you.

Fish are a good food source. If you do not have a fishing hook and line, use what you have to make them. You can use the string from your clothes for line. You can bend a small piece of metal like a hook. Insects and worms make good bait. You can also create a spear from a branch or use clothing as a net.

Sometimes people in the wilderness have supplies with them. It is important to keep supplies safe so they can be used.

Place food where animals cannot get it. Hang it high on a tree branch. If you cannot get the food into a tree, leave it at least 200 feet (61 m) from the campsite.

Hanging supplies between trees helps keep them away from bears and other animals.

Survivors need to take care of themselves. They should try to wash every day. If there is not enough water, they can take an "air bath." This is when a person takes off as much clothing as possible and lays it out in the sun. The air helps the skin. The sun kills bacteria. It is also important to keep your feet dry. Feet can develop bad sores if wet for too long.

There are things you can do to make it easier for rescuers to find you. Use signals in open areas. Move around to attract attention. Wave your arms and run back and forth. Make a lot of noise. Use a whistle if you have one. A sound repeated three times means someone needs help.

Planes flying above can see light cloth, even if it is dark out. Grayson had a bright yellow raincoat. He tore it into strips to mark the path he took. He waved the last piece over his head when he saw the rescuers.

Some people create signal fires. Adding green branches and leaves will make smoke that can be seen for miles on a clear day. The fire will be easy to see on **overcast** days and at night. But be sure to keep your signal fire under control.

You can also use a mirror to signal for help. Glass and metal can flash the sun's light for miles.

AVOIDING BAD BACTERIA

Bacteria are tiny organisms. You can only see them with a microscope. They live on food, plants, animals, and even people. Some bacteria are helpful. They help you **digest** food. But other bacteria can make you sick. Washing your hands is one of the best ways to get rid of bad bacteria. It is worth it to wash with water even if you do not have soap.

Bright colors and movement are easy to see from above.

Signals on the ground can help, too. Use clothing or branches to make shapes on the ground. They will look out of place to people flying above.

The wilderness can seem like a dangerous place. But people of all ages have survived in it. They learned the importance of being prepared and never giving up.

Glossary

damp (damp) Something is damp when it contains a small amount of liquid. Dew makes the ground feel damp.

digest (dye-JEST) To digest is to change food into a simpler form so it can be used by the body. The body must digest food to get more energy.

evergreen (EV-ur-green) An evergreen is a tree that has leaves that stay green all year. A pine tree is an evergreen tree.

hydrated (HYE-dray-ted) When something has enough water, it is hydrated. People must be hydrated to stay healthy.

insulation (in-suh-LAY-shuhn) Insulation is material used to prevent something from losing heat. Leaves, bark, grass, and hay can be used as insulation.

overcast (OH-vur-kast) The sky is overcast when it is very cloudy. An overcast sky hides the sun.

persimmons (pur-SIM-uhns) Persimmons are orange fruits that resemble plums. Persimmons are bitter before they are ripe.

purify (PYOOR-uh-fye) To purify is to make something clean. When you purify water, you get rid of bacteria.

ravine (ruh-VEEN) A ravine is a small, narrow valley with steep sides. You must be very careful if you hike near a ravine.

snowdrift (SNOH-drift) A snowdrift is a bank or pile of windblown snow. You can dig deep into a snowdrift for shelter.

To Learn More

BOOKS

All About Survival: 250 Facts Kids Want to Know. New York: TIME for Kids, 2014.

George, Jean Craighead, Twig C. George. *Pocket Guide to the Outdoors: Based on My Side of the Mountain*. New York: Dutton, 2009.

Long, Denise. *Survivor Kid: A Practical Guide to Wilderness Survival*. Chicago: Chicago Review Press, 2011.

McNab, Chris. *The Boy's Book of Outdoor Survival: 101 Courageous Skills for Exploring the Dangerous Wild*. Berkeley: Ulysses Press, 2008.

WEB SITES

Visit our Web site for links about how to survive in the wilderness:

childsworld.com/links

Note to Parents, Teachers, and Librarians: We routinely verify our Web links to make sure they are safe and active sites. So encourage your readers to check them out!

Index

5041